EVANGELINE EVERSHINE

and the

Case of the Biggest Disappearance Imaginable

PAGE PUBLISHING, INC.
Conneaut Lake, PA

First originally published by Page Publishing 2020

ISBN 978-1-6624-0857-1 (pbk)
ISBN 978-1-6624-0858-8 (digital)

Printed in the United States of America

Dedication

I dedicate this book to my wonderful family: my lovely, beautiful and encouraging wife, Teresa, my ambitious and personable daughter, Erica, another beauty, and her also ambitious and bright husband, Pete, their most wonderful, athletic and enterprising twins, gorgeous Eloise (Weezy) and handsome William, my determined and understanding son, Dean and his wise, dedicated, energetic and mature wife, Hanni, and their eight incomparable children, Bethany, Leah, Madeline, Rebekah, David, Hannah, Nathan and Aaron. AND my three (so far) inspiring great-grandchildren, Havilah, Eveline and Elijah.

Al Shapiro

EVANGELINE EVERSHINE

and the

Case of the Biggest Disappearance Imaginable

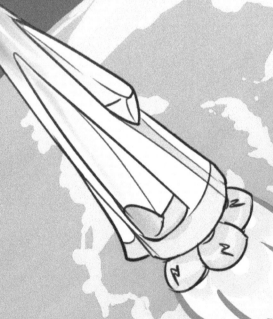

Al Shapiro

This is the story of Evangeline Evershine and how she solved a very intriguing mystery. The mystery happened every day. Every night, something disappeared, but it always returned the next day. This was no ordinary problem, but as we shall find, Evangeline was no ordinary girl. She was determined to solve this incredible case once and for all!

It was the sun that disappeared every night, only to return the next day. Evangeline wondered—where does the sun hide for the night? Where does it go? Why does it always come back in the morning?

Evangeline was only a young girl, but she could do things you and I can't. Her father, Mr. Evershine, was an astronaut, who flew spaceships high into the sky. Evangeline asked her father to take her on a spaceship to the sun to see where the sun went. Mr. Evershine, being a good and loving father, agreed.

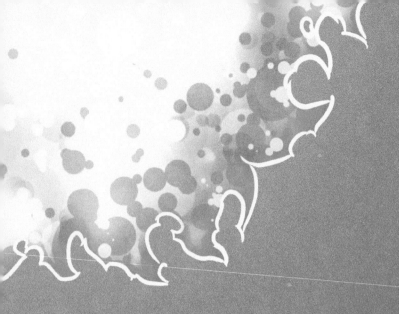

So one day, Evangeline and her father both put on their space suits, climbed into their spaceship, and blasted off. Once they were high up in the sky and they had left earth behind, they directed their spaceship toward the sun. Their spaceship traveled very fast—much, much faster than the fastest airplane.

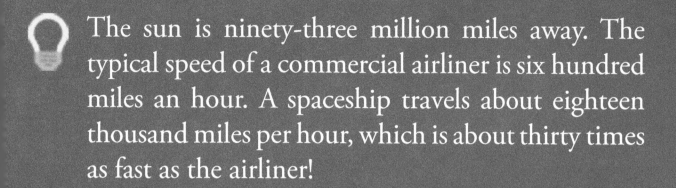

The sun is ninety-three million miles away. The typical speed of a commercial airliner is six hundred miles an hour. A spaceship travels about eighteen thousand miles per hour, which is about thirty times as fast as the airliner!

The sun is a hundred times as large as the earth.

The first day the sun was very bright, and it stayed bright in the morning, in the afternoon, in the evening—and even all night long. It was the second day and the third and the fourth. The sun never went away. It just stayed in the same place all the time! It never moved—it never disappeared.

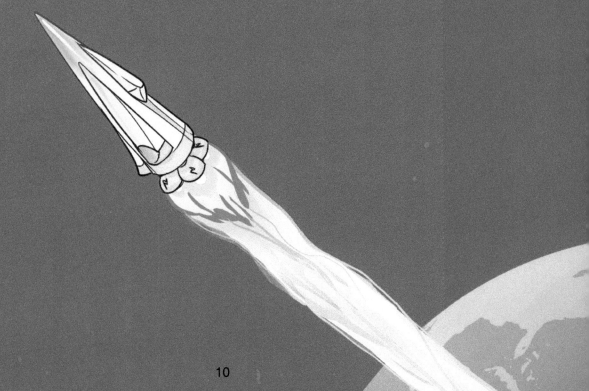

11

Then why did the sun disappear every night when
Evangeline was at home on earth?

Evangeline thought that maybe the answer was closer to earth. So she and her father turned their spaceship back toward earth and hurtled through space again.

As they approached the earth, Evangeline noticed something interesting: the earth was turning ever so slowly but nonetheless turning. It looked like a huge ball turning, turning, turning…it just kept turning and rotating day and night.

The earth rotates once each day. The sun takes twenty-four days to rotate once.

As the earth rotated, one side faced the sun and was all lit up by the sun and was very bright. The other side of the earth faced away from the sun and was pitch-black. So as the earth rotated, the part of the earth facing the sun was always changing very slowly.

Mystery solved! Being on earth in the daytime means you're on the part of the earth facing toward the sun.

But as the earth turns and nighttime comes, you're on the part of the earth facing away from the sun.

Evangeline and her father now headed back
to their spaceship landing dock back home.
Mission accomplished!

For Creative Minds!

The sun is a hundred times as large as the earth.

The sun is always radiating and beaming light.

The earth is constantly rotating around its axis, similar to but much, much slower than the wheel of a moving car. It takes twenty-four hours—or one whole day—for the earth to complete one rotation.

The sun also rotates, but its rotation is even slower than that of the earth. It takes twenty-four days, or almost a month, for the sun to rotate once.

As the earth rotates, half of the earth faces the sun while the other half faces away from the sun. And as the earth rotates, these two halves are constantly moving. Picture a rotating ball near a lamp. The half of the earth that faces the sun is illuminated by the sun, and this is known as daytime.

The half of the earth that faces away from the sun gets none of the sun's illumination, so this half of the earth is dark, and this is known as nighttime.

While rotating around its axis, the earth also revolves—or circles—around the sun. One full revolution of the earth around the sun takes one year.

The sun, on the other hand, stays in one place—it does not revolve.

The sun is ninety-three million (93,000,000) miles from earth.

Commercial airplanes fly at an average speed of about six hundred miles an hour. A spaceship travels at a speed of about eighteen thousand miles per hour, or about thirty times as fast.

Questions

1. How long do you think it would take the airplane or the spaceship to reach the sun?
2. Light travels at a speed of 186,000 miles per second. How long do you think it takes for the light of the sun to reach the earth?

Answers

1. To reach the sun, it would take an airplane more than seventeen years and a spaceship more than seven months.
2. The light of the sun takes a little over eight minutes to reach the earth.

Earth

One Day for the Earth to
Rotate Once Around Its Axis

93,000,000 miles

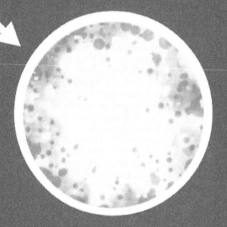

Sun

365 Days for the Earth to Revolve Once Around the Sun

About the Author

Al Shapiro is not a typical author. He is an electronics engineer who, upon graduating from college, was invited into two honorary scholastic engineering fraternities. He has two patents to his credit and has always had a deep interest in space.

He has twin grandchildren, William and Eloise, who are in elementary school. He frequently buys books for them and often reads these books to them at their bedtime and observes their reactions. This inspired him to write a children's book but of a different character—one that would not only be entertaining but also educational, one that would make learning fun. And so with his lifelong interest in space, that's the subject of this book, written for young children in a manner that will interest and amuse them, educate them, and stimulate them to learn more.

9 781662 408571